GUST

Written by
Katie Meyer

Illustrated by
Brigid Malloy

I am a wind turbine who lives above a port.

GUST

Written by
Katie Meyer

Illustrated by
Brigid Malloy

Ports help move things people need
between land and water.

I can see a lot from up here.
Ships, trains, and trucks come
through the port every day.

Everyone has a job to help the port run.
I want to help, too, but I don't know how.

On the pier, I see a lighthouse.
Lighthouses help by shining their light
high and low.

I want to help, too, but I cannot shine light.

In the water, I see a tugboat.
Tugboats help by moving other boats
back and forth.

I want to help, too, but I cannot move boats.

At the dock, I see a ship.
Ships help by hauling things
here and there.

I want to help, too, but I cannot float.

Across the port, I see a crane.
Cranes help by carrying containers
up and down.

I want to help, too, but I cannot lift containers.

On the tracks, I see a train.
Trains help by bringing cargo
in and out.

I want to help, too, but I cannot pull train cars.

On the road, I see a truck.
Trucks help by delivering goods
near and far.

I want to help, too, but I cannot drive.

Oh, look!

On the shore, I see the Port Director.
He directs everyone
left and right.

I see him help the ships, trains, and trucks.
Maybe he can help me!

Mr. Port Director, is there a job for me?

I cannot do what everyone else does.
How can I help?

Gust, my friend, you are helping, too.
You worked all day while the wind blew.

Your blades spin 'round while you stand tall,
to help make power for us all.

Look all around now that it's night,
the work you do creates our light!

You did!

There is a job for everyone.
Working together gets things done.

Now it is time for you to rest.
We need sleep to be at our best.

Good night, Gust.

Good night, port.

Good night, you!

That's me!

Gust is inspired by the sole wind turbine at Port Milwaukee. On the shore of Lake Michigan, the 100-kilowatt wind turbine stands 154 feet tall – less than half the height of most larger turbines! Despite its size, the turbine provides more than 100% of the electricity for the port and is the first to power a Milwaukee city building with clean, renewable electricity. Not only does it produce enough clean power for the port's headquarters, but its surplus energy is provided back to the city's power grid and can power up to 18 average Wisconsin homes.

CPSIA information can be obtained
at www.ICGtesting.com
Printed in the USA
JSHW051656240323
39315JS00001B/1